ROWAN
FELTED COLLECTION

A collection of 17 accessory designs by Sarah Hatton

Ford Felted Bag
page 6

Embrace Bag
page 8

Leah Corsage
page 10

Layla Corsage
page 10

Click Knitting Wrap
page 12

Pop Bag
page 14

Sophia Bracelets
page 16

Jessie Ribbon Bag
page 18

Ford Felted Purse
page 18

Clack Knitting Bag
page 20

Liberty Belt
page 22

Pippa Bag
page 22

Sula Slippers
page 24

Sula Slippers
page 24

Andi Messenger Bag
page 26

Ember Hot Water Bottle Cover *page 28*

Coddle Cushions
page 30

Aura Bag
page 32

Ford Felted Bag

YARN
SCOTTISH TWEED ARAN
A – Storm Grey 004   4 x 100 gm
B – Midnight 023   1 x 100 gm

NEEDLES
1 pair 5mm (no 6) (US 8) needles

EXTRAS
1 press fastener (optional)

TENSION
16 sts and 23 rows to 10cm over st st before washing.

BACK
Using A cast on 65 sts.
Working in st st throughout and starting with a K row, inc 1 st at each end of 3rd and 2 foll rows, then on 3 foll alt rows. 77 sts.
Cont without shaping, until Back meas 30cm, ending with a WS row. **
Work 4 rows more.
Change to B and knit 3 rows in garter st.
Cast off knitways (on WS).

FRONT
Work as given for Back to **
Next row. K3, * K2tog, yfwd, K2, rep from * to last 2 sts, K2.
Starting with a P row, work 3 rows.
Change to B and knit 3 rows in garter st.
Cast off knitways (on WS).

POCKET
Using A cast on 65 sts.
Starting with a K row, working in st st throughout, work 42 rows of pattern as set on chart AT SAME TIME inc 1 st at each end of 3rd and 2 foll rows, then on 3 foll alt rows.
77 sts.
Working in B, knit 3 rows in garter st.
Cast off knitways (on WS).

STRAP
Using A cast on 15 sts.
Work in st st until strap meas 197cm, ending with a WS row.
Cast off.

MAKING UP
Sew WS of pocket in place to RS of front of bag, matching cast on edges.
Join cast on and cast off edges of strap. With this seam at centre lower edge of bag, sew strap in place all round lower edge and sides of Front leaving centre section of strap loose to form handle. Sew strap to back in same way.
Machine wash at 60 degrees.

Using B make 2 twisted cords each 50cm long. Feed twisted cords through eyelets as in photograph and fasten at side edges. Make 2 pompons each approx. 5cm and attach to ends of cords. If necessary sew a press fastener to centre of cast off edge of pocket to make more secure.

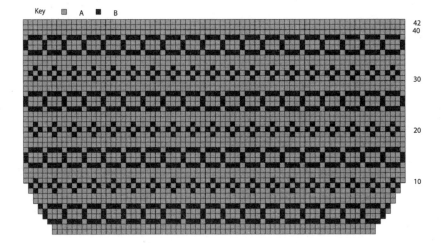

Key   □ A   ■ B

YARN
KID CLASSIC
2 x 50gm
(photographed in Lavender Ice 841)
Oddments of contrast yarn – 4 ply Soft in Victoria 390,
Clover 396 and Fairy 395

NEEDLES
1 pair 4½ mm (no 7) (US 7) needles

TENSION
22 sts and 28 rows to 10cm over st st on 4½ mm
needles before washing.

FIRST SIDE (BACK)
Cast on 46 sts.
Starting with a knit row and working in st st
(throughout) inc 1 st at each end of 3rd and 5 foll rows,
then on 4 foll alt rows. 66 sts.
Work 2 rows, ending with RS facing for next row.
Inc 1 st at each end of next and foll 3rd row, then on foll
4th row. 72 sts.
Work 24 rows without shaping, ending with a WS row.
Dec 1 st at each end of next and foll 4th row, then on 2
foll 3rd rows. 64 sts.
Work 4 rows, ending with RS facing for next row.
Dec 1 st at each end of next and 2 foll 4th rows, then on
4 foll 3rd rows. 50 sts.
Shape 1st handle
Next row(RS): K23, turn and leave rem sts on a holder,
working on these 23 sts only proceed as follows:-
Work 1 row.
Dec 1 st at each end of next and foll 3rd row then on foll
alt row. 17 sts.
Work 1 row.
Dec 1 st at end of next and at same side on foll 5th row,
then on 2 foll 4th rows. 13 sts.
Work 6 rows, ending with WS facing for next row.

Inc 1 st at beg of next row AT SAME TIME dec 1 st at
end of next and at same side of foll 5th row. 12 sts.
Work 6 rows, ending with WS facing for next row.
Next row: Inc 1 st at beg of row and dec 1 st at end of
row. 12 sts.
Work 6 rows, ending with RS facing for next row.
Cast off.
Shape 2nd handle
With RS facing, rejoin yarn to rem sts, cast off 8 sts and
knit to end. 19 sts.
Work 1 row.
Dec 1 st at each end of next and foll 3rd row then on foll
4th row. 13 sts.
Work 3 rows, ending with WS facing for next row.
Dec 1 st at beg of next row. 12 sts.
Work 3 rows, ending with WS facing for next row.
Inc 1 st at beg of next and at same side on 2 foll 3rd
rows and foll 4th row AT SAME TIME dec 1 st at end of
next and at same side on 2 foll 3rd rows and 2 foll alt
rows. 11 sts.
Work 1 row, ending with WS facing for next row.
Cast off.

SECOND SIDE (FRONT)
Work as given for first side, working in reverse stocking
stitch throughout.

MAKING UP
With K side of both sections outermost, join around
lower and side edges, beginning and ending in line with
start of strap shaping. Sew corresponding cast off edges
of handles together.
Using 1st contrast and chain stitch embroider around
open edges.
Using lazy daisy stitch embroider flowers of various
sizes in each of the contrast colours, as shown in photo.

Machine wash at 60 degrees.

Leah Corsage (shown on right)

YARN
KID CLASSIC

A – Spruce 853   1 x 50 gm
B – Lavender Ice 841   1 x 50 gm
C – Victoria 852   1 x 50 gm

NEEDLES
1 pair 4½ mm (no 7) (US 7) needles

EXTRAS
Embroidery threads in 2 colours.
Brooch back or safety pin to attach.

TENSION
22 sts and 28 rows to 10cm over st st on 4½ mm
needles before washing.

Using A cast on 28 sts and work in st st for 11cm.
Cast off.

Using B cast on 17 sts and work in st st for 9cm.
Cast off.

Using C cast on 17 sts and work in st st for 9cm.
Cast off.

MAKING UP
Machine wash all pieces at 60 degrees. Cut oval shape in
piece worked in colour A. Cut circles of varying sizes out
of pieces worked in colours B and C. Using embroidery
thread in a contrast colour sew 'spokes' on each circle as
shown in photograph. Attach circles to oval.
Attach pin to back of corsage.

Layla Corsage (shown on left)

YARN
KID CLASSIC

A – Victoria 852   1 x 50 gm
B – Spruce 853   1 x 50 gm
C – Lavender Ice 841   1 x 50 gm

NEEDLES
1 pair 4½ mm (no 7) (US 7) needles

EXTRAS
13 blue crystal beads ref CGB9 col. 58, 4 purple crystal
beads ref CGB9 col.10 and 11 pink crystal beads ref
CGB9 col. 8, all from Creative Bead Craft Ltd.
Brooch back or safety pin to attach.

TENSION
22 sts and 28 rows to 10cm over st st on 4½ mm
needles before washing.

Using A cast on 25 sts and work in st st for 13cm.

Cast off.

Using B cast on 28 sts and work in st st for 14cm.
Cast off.

Using C cast on 18 sts and work in st st for 10cm.
Cast off.

MAKING UP
Machine wash all pieces at 60 degrees. Using templates
as a guide cut out all pieces (template 1 using A, 2 and 3
using B and 4 using C). Stitch together as shown in
photograph and attach beads using blue crystal beads to
inside edge of 'flower' and remaining beads at random
on outer petal.

Attach pin to back of corsage.

See page 35 for template.

Click Knitting Wrap

YARN
TAPESTRY

4 x 50 gm
(photographed in Antique 173)

NEEDLES
1 pair 4mm (no 8) (US 6) needles

EXTRAS
2 x 1 metre lengths of ribbon

TENSION
22 sts and 30 rows to 10cm over st st on 4mm needles before washing.

Cast on 103 sts.
Starting with a knit row and working in st st

(throughout) cont until work meas 19cm, ending with a RS row.
Next row (WS) Knit (to form ridge).
Starting with a K row cont in st st until work meas 76cm, ending with a RS row.
Next row (WS) Knit (to form ridge).
Starting with a K row cont in st st until work meas 86cm, ending with a WS row.
Cast off.

MAKING UP
Fold lower edge at ridge point and sew at side edges. Sew lines down these section approx. 4cm apart to form pockets for needles. The top section (from the 2nd ridge to cast off will fold over to protect the top of your needles). Machine wash at 50 degrees. Sew ribbons on to form ties as shown.

Pop Bag

YARN
BIG WOOL
A – Glamour 036   5 x 100 gm
B – Zing 037   2 x 100 gm

NEEDLES
1 pair 10mm (no 000) (US15) needles

BUTTONS – 4

TENSION
9 sts and 12.5 sts to 10cm over st st on 10mm needles before washing

BACK AND FRONT (Both alike)
Cast on 17 sts using yarn A.
Row 1 (WS). Purl.
Row 2 (RS). K1, (inc in next st) twice, knit to last 3 sts, (inc in next st) twice, K1. 21 sts.
Row 3. P1, (inc in next st) twice, purl to last 3 sts, (inc in next st) twice, P1.
Row 4. As row 1.
Row 5. P1, inc in next st, purl to last 2 sts, inc in next st, P1.
Row 6. K1, inc in next st, knit to last 2 sts, inc in next st, K1. 33 sts.
Rows 5 and 6 set increasing.
Inc 1 st as set at each end of next 4 rows, then on every foll alt row to 51 sts.
Inc 1 st as set at each end of 2 foll 4th rows. 55 sts.
Work 19 rows without shaping.
Shape handle
Next row (RS). K24, turn and leave rem sts on a holder, cont as follows on these sts only-
Next row (WS). P1, P2tog, purl to end. 23 sts.
Working decs as set, dec 1 st at side edge in next row only AT SAME TIME dec 1 st at inner edge in next 4 rows.
18 sts.
Work 1 row.

Next row (WS). Dec 1 st as set at each end of row. 16 sts.
Work 4 rows without shaping, ending with RS facing for next row.
Dec 1 st as set at side edge only in next and 2 foll alt rows. 13 sts .
Work 3 rows dec 1 st at side edge and inc 1 st at handle edge in next and foll alt row. 13 sts.
Work 4 rows dec 1 st at side edge in next and foll alt row and at same time inc 1 st at handle edge in every row. 15 sts.
Break off yarn, leave rem sts on a holder.
Rejoin yarn to rem sts, cast off 7 sts, knit to end.
Complete to match first side of bag, reversing all shapings.
Break off yarn.
Rejoin yarn to first side of bag – K1, K2tog, knit to end, cast on 11 sts, then working across sts from second side, knit to last 3 sts, K2tog, K1. 39 sts.
Dec 1 st as set at each end of next 5 rows. 29 sts.
Next row (RS). K1, (K2tog) twice, knit to last 5 sts, (K2tog) twice, K1. 25 sts.
Next row. P1, (P2tog) twice, purl to last 5 sts, (P2tog) P1. 21 sts.
Dec 1 st as set at each end of next 2 rows. 17 sts.
Cast off rem 17 sts.

GUSSET
Cast on 15 sts using yarn B.
Work in st st for 96cm.

Pin centre of gusset to centre of cast on edge of back and front. Pin remainder of gusset in place around edges of front and back. Sew gusset in position.
Machine wash at 50 degrees.
Press out bag and leave to dry.
Make buttonholes by cutting 2 slits in each side of front as in photograph, the lower buttonholes approx. 5cm up from top of gusset.
Sew buttons in position on WS of back.

Sophia Bracelets

YARN
Purple beaded version
BIG WOOL Lucky 020   1 x 100 gm
Dark purple edged version
A – BIG WOOL W. Berry 025   1 x 100 gm
B – BIG WOOL FUSION Smokey 007   1 x 100 gm
Burgundy version
BIG WOOL Mulberry 042   1 x 100 gm

CROCHET HOOK
12mm (US U) crochet hook

EXTRAS
Variety of glass beads for beaded bracelet.

UK CROCHET ABBREVIATIONS
ch=chain; ss=slip stitch; dc=double crochet; tr=treble.

US CROCHET ABBREVIATIONS
ch=chain; ss=slip stitch; dc=single crochet; tr=double.

Using 12mm hook make 23 ch and join with a ss.

Purple beaded version
Work 1 ch, 1 round of dc and join with a ss, 2 ch then in same way as first round work, 2 rounds of tr, 1 ch and 1 round of dc. Fasten off.

Dark purple edged version
Working in same way as given for Purple beaded version work, 1 ch, 1 round of dc in A, 2 ch, 1 round of tr in B, 1 ch, and 1 round of dc in A. Fasten off.

Burgundy version
Work as given for dark purple version, using 1 colour throughout.

MAKING UP
Machine wash at 60 degrees, and decorate as desired.

Jessie Ribbon Bag

YARN
TAPESTRY
5 x 50 gm
(photographed in Leadmine 177)

NEEDLES
1 pair 4mm (no 8) (US 6) needles

EXTRAS
Piece of ribbon approx. 245cm long.

TENSION
22 sts and 30 rows to 10cm over st st on 4mm needles before washing.

BACK AND FRONT (one piece)
Cast on 99 sts.
Starting with a K row, work in st st until bag

meas 110 cm.
Cast off.

MAKING UP
Fold work in half matching cast on and cast off edges. Join side seams.
Machine wash at 50 degrees.
Mark a line down each side of bag, back and front, approx 6cm in from side edge. Cut 7 horizontal slits at each side, back and front, starting at the marked lines and cutting the width of the ribbon. Starting at top of slits and from WS, weave ribbon through one full line of slits, carrying ribbon under bag on RS at fold (as shown in photograph), then repeat through remaining line of slits.
Join the ends of the ribbon together once it has been fed through all slits.
Stitch the handles in place at top of bag.

Ford Felted Purse

YARN
SCOTTISH TWEED ARAN
A – Storm Grey 004   1 x 50 gm
B – Midnight 023   1 x 50 gm

NEEDLES
1 pair 5mm (no 6) (US 8) needles

EXTRAS
Zip to fit

TENSION
16 sts and 23 sts to 10cm over st st on 5mm needles before washing.

BACK
Using A and 5mm needles cast on 29 sts.

Work 20 rows in st st, ending with a WS row.
Change to B and knit 3 rows in garter st.
Cast off knitways (on WS).

FRONT
Using A and 5mm needles cast on 29 sts.

Work next 17 rows as shown on chart which is worked using the fair isle method.
Using A only, work 3 rows.
Change to B and knit 3 rows in g st.
Cast off knitways (on WS).

MAKING UP
Sew cast on edges together. Join side seams. Machine wash at 60 degrees.
Sew in zip.

Key

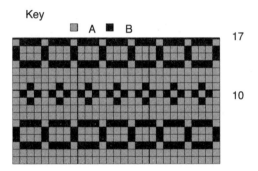

Clack Knitting Bag

YARN
LITTLE BIG WOOL
                    7 x 50 gm
(Photographed in Amethyst 504)

NEEDLES
1 pair 9mm (no 00) (US 13) needles

EXTRAS
2 pieces of dowelling each 30cm long
approx. 30 x 01009 beads
Fabric paint

TENSION
11 sts and 15 rows to 10cm over st st on 9mm needles
before washing.

SIDES (Make 2)
Using 9mm needles cast on 45 sts.
Starting with a Knit row, work 9 rows in st st, ending
with a RS row.
Next row (WS): Knit (to form ridge).
Cast on 6 sts at beg of next 2 rows.
57 sts.
Continue as follows:-
Row 1 (RS): K6, sl 1, K43, sl 1, K6.
Row 2: Purl.
These 2 rows set patt.
Cont in patt until side meas 40cm from ridge, ending
with a WS row.

Cast off 6 sts at beg of next 2 rows.
45 sts.
Work 4 rows in st st.
Next row: K15, turn and leave rem sts on a holder.
Working on these 15 sts only dec 1 st at beg of next
and 4 foll rows then on foll alt row.
10 sts.
Work 10 rows without shaping, ending with a RS row.
Next row (WS): Knit (to from ridge).
Starting with a K row, work 10 rows.
Cast off.
Rejoin yarn to rem sts, cast off 15 sts, knit to end.
Complete to match first side, reversing all shaping.
MAKING UP
Join knitted side panels along cast on edges (base) and
row end edges (sides). Fold bag so that base/side seams
meet and row end edges of base match cast-on edges of
side gussets, and sew seams.
Fold handles over at upper ridge and sew in position
leaving side edges open to slip dowelling handle into
place later.
Machine wash at 50 degrees.
Leave to dry.
Make stencil of flower and using the fabric paint stencil
flower onto one side of bag. Sew beads in place at
centre of flower.
Slip dowelling into place and sew edges of handles
together to secure.

See page 34 for template.

YARN
KID CLASSIC
2 x 50gm
(photographed in Straw 851)

NEEDLES
1 pair 4mm (no 8) (US 6) double pointed needles OR automatic French knitting mill

EXTRAS
1 metre suede or suede effect ribbon

Cast on 4 sts.
Row 1 (RS). K4, * without turning slip these 4 sts to opposite end of needle and bring yarn to opposite end of work pulling it quite tightly across WS of work, K these 4 sts again, rep from * until 2 balls of yarn have been used.
Cast off.
ALTERNATIVELY work using the automatic French knitting mill.

MAKING UP
Machine wash at 60 degrees.
Cut work into 3 pieces of equal length. Fold all pieces in half. Starting approx 7 cm down from folded end, wind suede around all sections pulling tightly and glueing in place. Work 4 more suede sections in the same way. Leave to dry.

YARN
A – **KID CLASSIC** Straw 851   4 x 50 gm
B – **TAPESTRY** Pot pourri 172   1 x 50 gm

NEEDLES
1 pair 4mm (no 8) (US 6) needles
1 pair 4½ mm (no 7) (US 7) needles

EXTRAS – 1 pair 00403 bag handles

TENSION
22 sts and 28 rows to 10cm over st st using yarn A and 4½ mm needles before washing.

SIDES (BOTH ALIKE)
Cast on 84 sts using 4½mm needles and yarn A.
Starting with a knit row, work in st st (throughout) until side meas 51cm, ending with **WS** facing for next row.
Knit 4 rows in garter stitch.
Cast off knitways (**on WS**).

FLOWER DETAILS
Cast on 76 sts using 4mm needles and B.
Starting with a knit row, work in st st until piece meas 41cm, ending with RS facing for next row. Cast off.

MAKING UP
Join side and lower seams of sides, leaving approx 13cm open at top edges. Machine wash bag at 60 degrees. Machine wash flower detail piece at 50 degrees.
Cut flower shapes out of flower detail piece, along with 4 straight strips approx 3cm wide to attach bag handles. Sew around edges of shapes using either zig-zag stitch on your sewing machine or blanket stitch hand embroidery. Attach shapes to bag as shown. Attach bag handles, using strips of B, as shown in photograph.

Sula Slippers

SIZE

	Small	Large	
	(up to UK 3)	(up to UK 7)	

YARN
BIG WOOL

2 colour version

A – Smoky 007	1	1	x 100 gm
B – Smudge 019	2	3	x 100 gm

1 colour embroidered version

A – White Hot 001	3	4	x 100 gm

Oddments of **Kid Classic** in Cherry Red 847
and Spruce 853

NEEDLES
1 pair 10mm (no 000) (US15) needles

EXTRAS
2 leather/suede patches if required

TENSION
9 sts and 12.5 rows to 10cm over st st on 10mm needles

before washing.

2 COLOUR VERSION
Cast on 35 [41] sts using A.
Work 4 rows in g st.
Change to B.
Starting with a K row, work 23 [24] cm in st st, ending with RS facing for next row.
Divide for top of foot
Next row: K24 (28), turn, P13 [15], turn.
On these 13 [15] sts only and using A, work 22 [26] rows in st st, break yarn.
With RS facing and using B (and 11 [13] sts on needle), pick up and knit 11 [13] sts along side of centre panel extension, knit across 13 [15] sts from toe,
11 [13] sts along side of centre panel extension and K across rem 11 [13] sts on needle. 57 [67] sts.
Work 7 [8] cm in g st, ending with RS facing for next row.
Shape sole
Row 1: K1, * K2tog, K22 (27), K2tog * K3, work from * to * again, K1.
Row 2: K23 (28), K2tog, K3, K2tog, K to end.
Row 3: K1, *K2tog, K19 (24), K2tog * K3, work from * to * again. K1.
Row 4: K20 (25), K2tog, K3, K2tog, knit to end.
Row 5: K1, * K2tog, K16 (21), K2tog, * K3, work from * to * again, K1.
Row 6: K17 (22), K2tog, K3, K2tog, knit to end.
Row 7: K1, * K2tog, K13 (18), K2tog * K3, work from * to * again, K1.
Row 8: Cast off.

MAKING UP
Join leg and underfoot seam.
Machine wash at 50 degrees.
If slippers are to be worn rather than used as a decoration, sew a leather/suede patch to soles of boots.

1 COLOUR VERSION
Work as given for 2 colour version using A throughout.

MAKING UP
Join leg and underfoot seam. Using couching and lazy daisy stitch embroider boots as shown.
Machine wash at 50 degrees.
If required sew a leather/suede patch to soles of boots.

YARN
SCOTTISH TWEED ARAN
Oatmeal   025   3 x 100 gm

NEEDLES
1 pair 5mm (no 6) (US 8) needles

BUTTONS
1 x 00339

TENSION
16 sts and 23 rows to 10cm over st st on 5mm needles before washing.

MAIN PIECE
Cast on 59 sts.
Knit 4 rows in garter st.
Starting with a Knit row, work in st st until work meas 35cm, ending with a RS row.
Next row: (WS) Knit (to form ridge).
Work 17 rows, ending with a RS row.
Next row: (WS) Knit (to form ridge).
Cont in st st until work meas 35cm from second ridge, ending with **WS** facing for next row.
Next row: (WS) Knit (to form ridge).
Cont in st st until work meas 26cm from third ridge, ending with **WS** facing for next row.
Knit 4 rows.
Cast off knitways (**on WS**).

STRAP
Cast on 16 sts.

Row 1 (RS): K3, * P2, K2, rep from * to last st, K1.
Row 2: K1, * P2, K2, rep from * to last 3 sts, P2, K1.
These 2 rows set rib and garter stitch.
Cont in patt as set until strap meas 175cm, ending with RS facing for next row.
Cast off in patt.

POCKET
Cast on 28 sts.
Row 1 (RS): K3, * P2, K2, rep from * to last st, K1.
Row 2: K1, * P2, K2, rep from * to last 3 sts, P2, K1.
These 2 rows set rib and garter stitch.
Cont in patt as set until pocket meas 13cm, ending with RS facing for next row.
Next row: Patt 13, cast off 2 sts, patt to end.
Next row: Patt 13, cast on 2 sts, patt to end.
Work 4 rows more in patt.

MAKING UP
Sew cast on and cast off edges of straps in position to section between first two ridges and sew selvedges of straps to side selvedges of bag, ending at cast on edge and third ridge to form sides of bag, leaving the middle section loose to form strap and the remaining section of bag to form flap.
Sew pocket in position as shown.
Machine wash at 60 degrees.
Sew on button.
Press and leave to dry.

Ember Hot Water Bottle Cover

YARN
SCOTTISH TWEED DK

A – Thistle 016	1 x 100 gm
B – Purple Heather 030	1 x 100 gm
C – Indigo 031	1 x 100 gm
D – Porridge 024	1 x 100 gm

NEEDLES
1 pair 4mm (no 8) (US 6) needles

EXTRAS
3 x 00318 buttons

TENSION
20 sts and 28 rows to 10cm over st st on 4mm before washing.

BACK AND FRONT (Both Alike)
Using 4mm needles and A cast on 65 sts.
Starting with a K row, working in st st, work as given for chart until chart row 76 has been completed, ending with RS facing for next row.
Using yarn D, work 58 rows in st st, ending with RS facing for next row.
Using A cast off.

To Make Up
Join cast edges and side seams, leaving approx. 11cm open at top on each side seam.
Machine wash at 60 degrees.
On front piece – On cast off edge, place a marker approx. 9 cm in from each edge and cut a diagonal line down from this point to top of side seam. Using A, blanket stitch around edges as shown. (You may wish to wash your work again at 50 degrees to felt these sts).
Sew a button on WS centre back approx. 1 cm below cast off edge, in centre of top section and 1 on RS of front on each diagonal approx halfway down. Cut buttonholes to match.

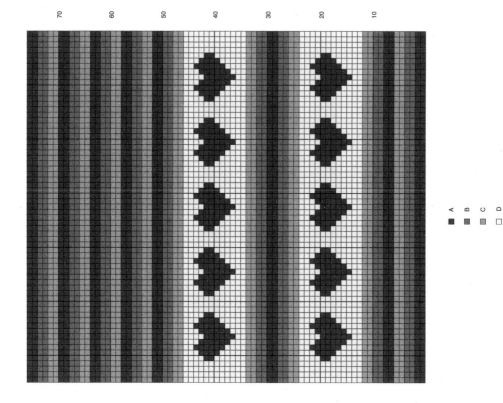

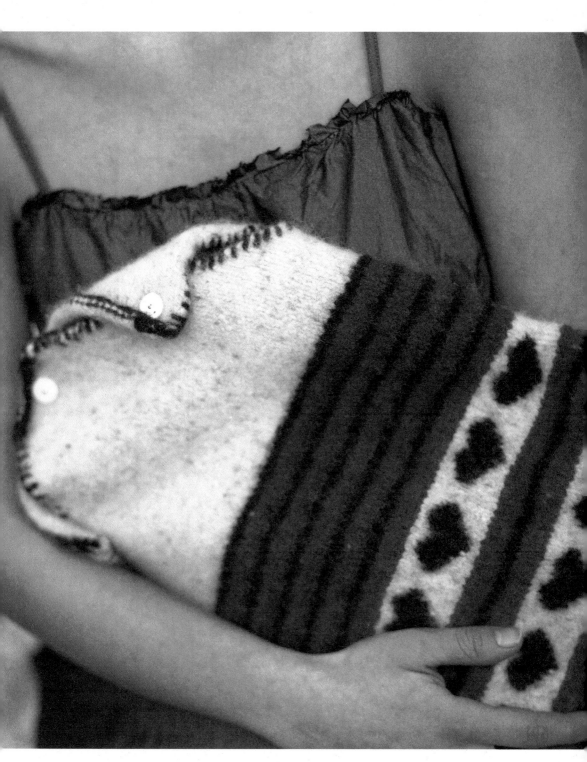

YARN

Cabled version
KID CLASSIC   9 x 50 gm
Photographed in Crystal 840

Beaded version
KID CLASSIC   9 x 50 gm
Photographed in Smoke 831

NEEDLES
1 pair 4½ mm (no 7) (US 7) needles

EXTRAS (for beaded version only)
115 beads ref SB5 col 1 silver from Creative Bead Craft Ltd.

TENSION
22 sts and 28 rows to 10cm over st st on 4½ mm
needles before washing.

Special abbreviations
C12B – slip next 6 sts onto a cable needle and hold at back
of work, knit next 6 sts then knit sts from cable needle.
Bead 1 = place a bead by bringing yarn to RS of work
and slipping bead up next to st just worked, slip next st
purlwise from left needle to right needle and take yarn
to WS of work, leaving bead sitting in front on slipped st
on RS.

Pattern note (for beaded version)
Before starting to knit the beaded band, thread beads
onto yarn. To do this, thread a fine sewing needle (one
that will easily pass through the beads) with sewing
thread. Knot ends of thread and then pass end of yarn
through this loop. Thread a bead onto sewing thread and
then slide it along and onto knitting yarn. Continue in
this way until required number of beads are on yarn.

CUSHION FRONT (Both versions)
Cast on 131 sts.
Work in st st until piece meas 65cm, ending with
a RS row.
Knit 2 rows in garter st.
Cast off knitways on WS.

CUSHION BACK (Both versions)
Cast on 131 sts.
Work in st st until piece meas 106 cm, ending with
a RS row.
Knit 2 rows in garter st.

Cast off knitways on WS.

CABLED BAND (Cabled version only)
Cast on 16 sts.
Row 1 (RS). Knit.
Row 2. K2, P12, K2.
Rep last 2 rows once.
Row 5. K2, C12B, K2.
Row 6. As row 2.
Row 7 to 12. Rep row 1 and 2 3 times.
These 12 rows set pattern.
Cont in pattern until strip meas 60cm, ending with
a WS row.
Cast off.

BEADED BAND (Beaded version only)
Cast on 117 sts.
Knit 2 rows in garter st.
Work from chart row 1 to 19 (repeating 16 st repeat 7
times) as set on chart, ending with a RS row.
Knit 2 rows in garter st.
Cast off knitways (on WS).

MAKING UP
Join cast on edges of back and front. Join side seams up
to cast off edges of front piece, at same time catch
bands in position in side seam approx 15cm down from
this top edge. Machine wash at 60 degrees.

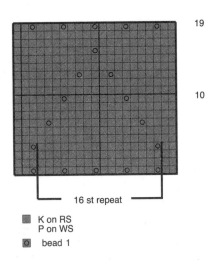

■ K on RS
   P on WS
◎ bead 1

Aura Bag

YARN
LITTLE BIG WOOL

7 x 50 gm

(photographed in Pearl 500)
Oddments of Jasper 505 and Garnet 503 for embroidery

NEEDLES
1 pair 9mm (no 00) (US 13) needles
1 pair 7mm (no 2) (US 10½) needles

TENSION
11 sts and 15 rows to 10cm over st st on 9mm needles before washing.

SIDES (Both alike and knitted from top to bottom)
Using 9mm needles cast on 45 sts.
Knit 4 rows in garter st.
Starting with a knit row and working in st st throughout cont until side meas 54cm, ending with WS facing for next row.
Next row (WS): Knit (to form ridge).
Cont in st st for 12 rows, inc 1 st at each end of 3rd and foll 4th row.
49 sts.
Knit 2 rows in garter st.
Cast off.

HANDLES (Both alike)
Using 7mm needles cast on 51 sts.
Knit 9 rows in garter st.
Cast off knitways.

MAKING UP
Join side edges, reversing seam from ridge to cast off edge. Turn this section back so that WS is now facing. Join lower edge of bag at the ridge row.
Using contrast yarns and chain stitch embroider 'double' circles on this turnback, and a line of each contrast approx. 2 cm apart just below garter st at top edge of bag as in photograph.
Join handles to top of bag, making each side of handle approx. 11cm apart.
Machine wash at 50 degrees.
Cut into centre of each double circle and remove fabric.

Clack Knitting Bag template

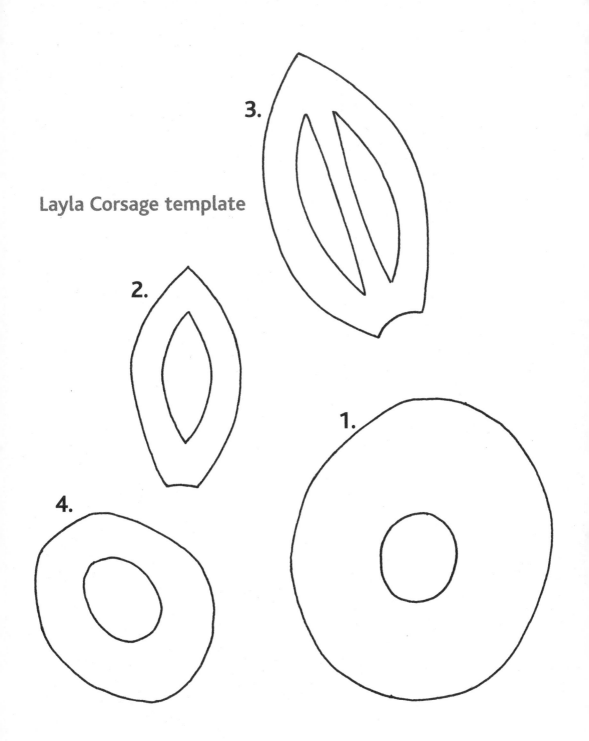

Layla Corsage template

3.

2.

1.

4.

Information

Tension

We recommend that you knit a square in pattern and/or stocking stitch (depending on the pattern instructions) of perhaps 5 - 10 more stitches and 5 - 10 more rows than those given in the tension note. Mark out the central 10cm square with pins. If you have too many stitches to 10cm try again using thicker needles, if you have too few stitches to 10cm try again using finer needles.

Felting in the Washing Machine

All of the projects featured within this collection are considered suitable for knitter's of all abilities. We have felted all of the pieces in the washing machine, making the results quick and easy. As all washing machines give slightly different results, you may wish to test the felting on your tension square before starting your project. We have suggested washing Kid Classic, Scottish Tweed DK & Aran at 60°C and all other yarns featured (Little Big Wool, Tapestry, Big Wool) at 50°C. You may also find that you get better results if you wash smaller projects with something bulky (i.e. old jeans) in the machine, bearing in mind colour may run.

Chart Note

Many of the patterns in the brochure are worked from charts. Each square on a chart represents a stitch and each line of squares a row of knitting. Each colour used is given a different letter and these are shown in the materials section, or in the key alongside the chart of each pattern. When working from the charts, read odd rows (K) from right to left and even rows (P) from left to right, unless otherwise stated.

Fairisle Technique

Fairisle type knitting: When two or three colours are worked repeatedly across a row, strand the yarn not in use loosely behind the stitches being worked. If you are working with more than two colours, treat the "floating" yarns as if they were one yarn and always spread the stitches to their correct width to keep them elastic. It is advisable not to carry the stranded or "floating" yarns over more than three stitches at a time, but to weave them under and over the colour you are working. The "floating" yarns are therefore caught at the back of the work.

Stitching

When stitching the pieces together, remember to match areas of colour and texture very carefully where they meet. Use a seam stitch such as back stitch or mattress stitch for all main knitting seams and join all ribs and neckband with mattress stitch, unless otherwise stated.

Abbreviations

K	- Knit	beg	- begin(ning)	patt	- pattern
P	- Purl	foll	- following	tog	- together
st(s)	- stitch(es)	rem	- remain(ing)	mm	- millimetres
inc	- increas(e)(ing)	rev st - st	- reverse stocking stitch	cm	- centimetres
dec	- decreas(e)(ing)		(1 row P, 1 row K)	in(s)	- inch(es)
st-st	- stocking Stitch	rep	- repeat	rs	- right side
	(1 row K, 1 row P)	alt	- alternate	ws	- wrong side
g st	- garter Stitch -	cont	- continue	meas	- measures
	(K every row)	sl1	- slip one stitch	yfwd	- yarn forward

AUSTRALIA:
Australian Country Spinners, 314 Albert Street,
Brunswick, Victoria 3056
Tel: (61) 3 9380 3888   Fax: (61) 3 9387 2674
E-mail: sales@auspinners.com.au

BELGIUM:
Pavan, Meerlaanstraat 73, B9860 Balegem (Oosterzele).
Tel: (32) 9 221 8594   Fax: (32) 9 221 8594
E-mail: pavan@pandora.be

CANADA:
Diamond Yarn, 9697 St Laurent, Montreal, Quebec, H3L 2N1
Tel: (514) 388 6188

Diamond Yarn (Toronto),
155 Martin Ross, Unit 3, Toronto, Ontario, M3J 2L9
Tel: (416) 736 6111 Fax: (416) 736 6112
E-mail: diamond@diamondyarn.com www.diamondyarn.com

DENMARK:
Coats Danmark A/S, Mariendlunds Alle 4, 7430 Ikast
Tel: (45) 96 60 34 00   Fax: (45) 96 60 34 08
Email: coats@coats.dk

FINLAND:
Coats Opti Oy, Ketjutie 3, 04220 Kerava
Tel: (358) 9 274 871   Fax: (358) 9 2748 7330
E-mail: coatsopti.sales@coats.com

FRANCE:
Coats France / Steiner Frères, 100, avenue du Général de Gaulle,
18 500 Mehun-Sur-Yèvre
Tel: (33) 02 48 23 12 30   Fax: (33) 02 48 23 12 40

GERMANY:
Coats GMbH, Kaiserstrasse 1, D-79341 Kenzingen
Tel: (49) 7644 8020   Fax: (49) 7644 802399
www.coatsgmbh.de

HOLLAND:
de Afstap, Oude Leliestraat 12, 1015 AW Amsterdam
Tel: (31) 20 6231445   Fax: (31) 20 427 8522

HONG KONG:
East Unity Co Ltd, Unit B2, 7/F Block B, Kailey Industrial Centre,
12 Fung Yip Street, Chai Wan
Tel: (852) 2869 7110   Fax: (852) 2537 6952
E-mail: eastuni@netvigator.com

ICELAND:
Storkurinn, Laugavegi 59, 101 Reykjavik
Tel: (354) 551 8258   E-mail: malin@mmedia.is

ITALY:
D.L. srl, Via Piave, 24 – 26, 20016 Pero, Milan
Tel: (39) 02 339 10 180   Fax: (39) 02 33914661

JAPAN:
Puppy Co Ltd, T151-0051, 3-16-5 Sendagaya, Shibuyaku, Tokyo
Tel: (81) 3 3490 2827   Fax: (81) 3 5412 7738
E-mail: info@rowan-jaeger.com

KOREA:
Coats Korea Co Ltd, 5F Kuckdong B/D, 935-40 Bangbae- Dong,
Seocho-Gu, Seoul
Tel: (82) 2 521 6262   Fax: (82) 2 521 5181

LEBANON:
y.knot, Saifi Village, Mkhalissiya Street 162, Beirut,
Tel: (961) 1 992211   Fax: (961) 1 315553
E mail: y.knot@cyberia.net.lb

NORWAY:
Coats Knappehuset AS, Pb 100 Ulste, 5873 Bergen
Tel: (47) 55 53 93 00 Fax: (47) 55 53 93 93

SINGAPORE:
Golden Dragon Store, 101 Upper Cross Street #02-51, People's
Park Centre, Singapore 058357
Tel: (65) 6 5358454   Fax: (65) 6 2216278
E-mail: gdscraft@hotmail.com

SOUTH AFRICA:
Arthur Bales PTY, PO Box 44644, Linden 2104
Tel: (27) 11 888 2401   Fax: (27) 11 782 6137

SPAIN:
Oyambre, Pau Claris 145, 80009 Barcelona.
Tel: (34) 670 011957   Fax: (34) 93 4872672
E-mail: oyambre@oyambreonline.com

SWEDEN:
Coats Expotex AB, Division Craft, Box 297, 401 24 Grteborg
Tel: (46) 33 720 79 00 Fax: 46 31 47 16 50

TAIWAN:
Laiter Wool Knitting Co Ltd, 10-1 313 Lane, Sec 3, Chung Ching
North Road, Taipei
Tel: (886) 2 2596 0269   Fax : (886) 2 2598 0619

Mon Cher Corporation, 9F No 117 Chung Sun First Road,
Kaoshiung.   Tel: (886) 7 9711988   Fax: (886) 7 9711666

U.S.A.:
Westminster Fibers Inc, 4 Townsend West, Suite 8,
Nashua, New Hampshire 03063
Tel: (1 603) 886 5041 / 5043   Fax (1 603) 886 1056
E-mail: rowan@westminsterfibers.com

U.K:
Rowan, Green Lane Mill, Holmfirth, West Yorkshire,
England HD9 2DX
Tel: +44 (0) 1484 681881   Fax: +44 (0) 1484 687920
E-mail: mail@knitrowan.com   Inernet: www.knitrowan.com

**For stockists in all other countries please contact Rowan for
stockist details.**

SELECTED STYLING FROM:
Saltwater
98 Marylebone Lane, London W1
Tel: 020 7935 3336
www.saltwater.net

Caravan
11 Lamb Street, Spitalfields, London E1 6EA
Tel: + 44 (0)20 7247 6467
www.caravanstyle.com

Notes